the old bridge

Published in the United States by Clarkson N. Potter, Inc., 225 Park Avenue South,
New York, New York 10003, and represented in Canada by the Canadian MANDA Group

Published in Great Britain by MacDonald and Co (Publishers) Ltd as
Bellamy's Changing World: The River

CLARKSON N. POTTER, POTTER, and colophon are trademarks of Clarkson N. Potter, Inc.

Conceived, edited, and produced by Frances Lincoln Limited,
Apollo Works, 5 Charlton Kings Road,
London NW5, England.

Manufactured in Italy

Library of Congress Cataloging-in-Publication Data

Bellamy, David J.
    The river.
    (Our changing world)
    Summary: Relates how plants and creatures co-exist
in a river and their struggle for survival when a
man-made catastrophe strikes.
    1. Stream ecology – Juvenile literature. [1. Stream ecology. 2. Ecology] I. Dow, Jill, ill. II. Title.
III. Series: Bellamy, David J. Our changing world.
QH541.5.S7B45 1988   574.5'26323   87-21837
ISBN 0-517-56801-2 (Crown)

10 9 8 7 6 5 4 3 2 1

First Edition

O U R
C H A N G I N G
W O R L D

The
RIVER

by DAVID BELLAMY
with illustrations by Jill Dow

Clarkson N. Potter, Inc./Publishers
DISTRIBUTED BY CROWN PUBLISHERS, INC., NEW YORK

This is a story about a river whose banks and water are home to many creatures. Lots of people enjoy it, too. It is a beautiful place, full of life and color.

Here it is in winter. Many birds have come to feed on the fruits of trees like the holly and the hawthorn.

Ducks, mink, and deer have left their tracks in the soft covering of snow at the icy river's edge.

Two ducks and a drake swim up to eat the crusts and grain that visitors have brought for them. A pike is looking for food, too. You won't see any frogs now: they stored their food as a layer of fat under their skin in autumn before they hibernated and they are all fast asleep in the mud in the shallows.

It's early summer now. From the new concrete bridge you can look down into the clear dark water and see the giant pike lying in wait among the waterweeds, beneath the storm overflow pipe from the food factory. The river is almost choked with water plants: rushes and sedges along the edge, and water-lilies and pondweeds nearer open water. A heron is looking for fish and frogs in the shallows. He has a nest in the old willow tree on the opposite bank from where a fisherman is casting his line.

Beside the river it is cool and damp. Swans and ducks swim up with their young, hoping to be fed. The air is buzzing with insects. The blue damsel-flies, resting on the rushes, spend much of their lives as rather ugly nymphs in the water. There they catch and eat other water insects, tadpoles, and even tiny fish, before emerging to fly free.

Scoop up some pond water in a shallow white bowl, and see what you catch. Don't leave the bowl in the sun, because the creatures will get too hot, and put them back quickly. Here is a stickleback with a row of little spikes on its back for protection, a water boatman usings its legs like oars, a pair of diving beetles, and a long waterstick insect.

1 dragonfly nymph 2 tadpoles
3 stickleback 4 water boatman
5 great diving beetle – female
6 great diving beetle – male
7 waterstick insect

The young fish in one of
the fisherman's long nets
are plant-eaters, while
the carp eats plants
and worms. The
eels in the other
net eat fish
and frogs.

The pike in this stretch of the river is so big it can eat all the other sorts of fish and even the ducklings. When the fisherman throws a handful of bait into the water to attract more fish, the drake flies in to enjoy a free meal.

Good fishermen always leave the river clean and tidy, taking home any broken line, hooks and weights that might maim or kill birds and other animals.

1 water snail 2 snails' eggs 3 froglet 4 water scorpion
5 water boatman 6 freshwater shrimp 7 pond skater
8 water strider

In the summer, when it's hot and dry, the river flows very slowly. When the sun is shining, all the green plants crowding the river make oxygen that bubbles into the water. Some creatures — like the pike and the freshwater shrimp — have gills which they use to "breathe" the oxygen they need. The froglets have lungs and so must swim up for gulps of air, although when they were tadpoles they, too, had gills. The water boatman collects air bubbles on its hairy abdomen and the water scorpion takes in air through a snorkel-like tail.

Some insects, like the pond skater and water strider, are so light they can walk or skim about on the surface of the water, and small black flat worms and water snails can move along hanging down from the surface. The snails stick their eggs onto the underside of the lily leaves where they won't dry up.

Some water plants have differently shaped leaves above and below water. The soft underwater leaves are ideal food for ducklings. Fortunately, the pike isn't here to see these two ducklings or the frogs.

1 arrowhead
2 mare's tail
3 sponge
4 hydra

All sorts of creatures live on the old brick wall. A spider has caught a damselfly in its web, and a mason wasp is laying her eggs in a crack. Under the water, a sponge, which is a very simple animal, sieves food from the water, while green hydra somersault along on their tentacles, and snails are eating watercress.

Here the river tumbles down an old dam and forms a riffle. Many creatures can live here because the falling water stirs in tiny bubbles of oxygen-rich air. The creatures have to hang on tightly, though, or they will be swept away.

1 mayfly   2 dragonfly   3 alderfly larva
4 limpet   5 caddisfly larva

The caddisfly larvae protect themselves with houses made of sticks and leaves, or tiny shells and stones. But when the larvae turn into adult insects they, like the gnats and mayflies, are easy prey for the frog. The dragonfly is out hunting the insects too.

The swallows swoop down to catch insects that have emerged from the water by the old stone bridge, and a water vole sticks its head out of a hole just above water level. Bees are buzzing around the Himalayan balsam. Bluetits are collecting the soft covering of cattails to line their nests, and a duck is calling one of her ducklings.

The old bridge is home to many living things. House martins have built their nests high up under the bridge, and butterflies sun themselves on the stonework. The ice-cream man always stops here, too. Some young visitors have crossed the bridge to buy cones from him and tell him about all the interesting things they've seen on the river.

But back at the new bridge
something terrible is
happening! Filthy waste is
pouring out of the pipe from
the factory into the river.

The fisherman has run off to sound the alarm.

The animals are getting away as fast as they can, fleeing from the suffocating stream of waste, but the fish and many of the small water creatures cannot escape.

The flow has been stopped, but too late. The damage has been done. The water is covered with dead fish, and the smell is terrible.

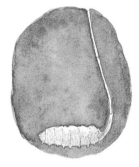

rat-tailed maggot

Bacteria, too small to see, are at work breaking down the waste, but to do this they use up all the oxygen in the water. Without oxygen to breathe, even the great pike and the eel can't survive. White sewage fungus, growing out of control in the polluted water, smothers the weeds. The only creatures that can thrive in the water are rat-tailed maggots, which breathe through a tail like a telescopic snorkel.

The frogs are all right, too, and sit on the bank feasting on the swarms of flies.

The black-headed gulls squabbling over their share of the dead fish are helping to clean up the mess.

Beyond the dam, at the riffle, things are better. The waste has been diluted, and the falling water stirs oxygen into the river, making it easier for river creatures to live. A small pike swims by and the mud between the stones is full of red bloodworms.

Tiny green plants called algae cover the rocks or trail in the
water — they, also, bubble oxygen into the water and help
make it clean again. The snails and ducks both like to eat
algae. The frogs are catching clouds of mosquitoes and
midges that have hatched out — you can see their empty
pupae, as well as some larvae, hanging down from the
surface of the water.

It is late summer now, almost a month since the disaster. The river is nearly back to normal, and everyone who enjoys walking by the water or sitting on the bank hopes the factory owners will be more careful in the future.

Under the old bridge, the river looks clean again. The water is a little greener from all the algae that are still growing, but sewage fungus no longer clogs the weeds. Frogs are croaking, and bats are flitting around catching insects. The duck is sitting on a new nest among the cattails. Although many fish have died, others have moved into this stretch, and the young pike is growing fast. Soon he will be the new king of the river.

the factory

the new bridge

the dam

the riffle